WYOMING

The Equality State

BY
JOHN HAMILTON

Abdo & Daughters
An imprint of Abdo Publishing | abdopublishing.com

abdopublishing.com

Published by ABDO Publishing, a division of ABDO, PO Box 398166, Minneapolis, Minnesota 55439. Copyright © 2017 by Abdo Consulting Group, Inc. International copyrights reserved in all countries. No part of this book may be reproduced in any form without written permission from the publisher. ABDO & Daughters™ is a trademark and logo of ABDO Publishing.

Printed in the United States of America, North Mankato, Minnesota.
082016
092016

Editor: Sue Hamilton   **Contributing Editor:** Bridget O'Brien
Graphic Design: Sue Hamilton
Cover Art Direction: Candice Keimig   **Cover Photo Selection:** Neil Klinepier
Cover Photo: iStock
Interior Images: Alamy, AP, Buffalo Bill Center of the West, Casper Area Economic Development Alliance, City of Gillette, Dreamstime, Getty, Granger Collection, Greg Goebel, iStock, John Hamilton, John Tronier, Kevin Cole, Library of Congress, Mile High Maps, Montana Historical Society/Edward S. Paxson, Mountain High Flags, Minden Pictures, National Gallery of Art/George Catlin, One Mile Up, Saratoga Museum, Science Source, U.S. Air Force, U.S. Geological Survey, University of Wyoming, W.H. Jackson, White House, Wyoming State Archives, & Wikimedia.

Statistics: *State and City Populations*, U.S. Census Bureau, July 1, 2015 estimates; *Land and Water Area*, U.S. Census Bureau, 2010 Census, MAF/TIGER database; *State Temperature Extremes*, NOAA National Climatic Data Center; *Climatology and Average Annual Precipitation*, NOAA National Climatic Data Center, 1980-2015 statewide averages; *State Highest and Lowest Points*, NOAA National Geodetic Survey.

Websites: To learn more about the United States, visit booklinks.abdopublishing.com. These links are routinely monitored and updated to provide the most current information available.

Cataloging-in-Publication Data
Names: Hamilton, John, 1959- author.
Title: Wyoming / by John Hamilton.
Description: Minneapolis, MN : Abdo Publishing, [2017] | Series: The United
    States of America | Includes index.
Identifiers: LCCN 2015957752 | ISBN 9781680783544 (lib. bdg.) |
    ISBN 9781680774580 (ebook)
Subjects: LCSH: Wyoming--Juvenile literature.
Classification: DDC 978.7--dc23
LC record available at http://lccn.loc.gov/2015957752

CONTENTS

THE
EQUALITY
STATE

Wyoming is a Western wonderland filled with windswept plains, soaring mountains, spouting geysers, roaming wildlife, and enough adventure to last a lifetime. It is the 10th-largest state, but it has the fewest people. That makes for many wide-open spaces, and plenty of acres for cattle to graze. Wyoming is a rugged yet beautiful land.

In the 1800s, Wyoming was a highway to the West. Near Guernsey, Wyoming, one can still see the ruts from the thousands of wagon wheels that ground into the soft sandstone rock. Later, the first transcontinental railroad was built across the state, connecting the East Coast with the West Coast. Today, instead of simply passing through, millions of visitors stay to experience Wyoming's natural beauty and its freedom-loving people.

In the late 1800s, Wyoming became the first state to grant women the right to vote. That is why Wyoming today is nicknamed "The Equality State."

A train rumbles through Wyoming, transporting products across the state.

QUICK FACTS

Name: The name "Wyoming" is a variation of two Delaware Native American words, "Mecheweai-Ing." It means "at the big plains," which early white settlers thought was appropriate for Wyoming.

State Capital: Cheyenne, population 63,335

Date of Statehood: July 10, 1890 (44th state)

Population: 586,107 (least-populous state)

Area (Total Land and Water): 97,813 square miles (253,335 sq km), 10th-largest state

Largest City: Cheyenne, population 63,335

Nicknames: The Equality State; Big Wyoming; The Cowboy State

Motto: Equal Rights

State Bird: Meadowlark

State Flower: Indian Paintbrush

State Gemstone: Jade

State Tree: Plains Cottonwood

State Song: "Wyoming"

Highest Point: Gannett Peak, 13,804 feet (4,207 m)

Lowest Point: Belle Fourche River, 3,099 feet (945 m)

Average July High Temperature: 82°F (28°C)

Record High Temperature: 115°F (46°C), Diversion Dam near Pavillion on July 15, 1988

Average January Low Temperature: 11°F (-12°C)

Gannett Peak

Record Low Temperature: -66°F (-54°C), Riverside Ranger Station in Yellowstone National Park on February 9, 1933

Average Annual Precipitation: 16 inches (41 cm)

Belle Fourche River

Number of U.S. Senators: 2

Number of U.S. Representatives: 1

U.S. Postal Service Abbreviation: WY

GEOGRAPHY

Wyoming is in the Western region of the United States. It is the 10th-largest state. It covers 97,813 square miles (253,335 sq km) of land. The state is shaped like a square. To the north is the state of Montana. Sharing borders to the west are Montana, Idaho, and Utah. To the south are Utah and Colorado. Bordering Wyoming to the east are the states of Nebraska and South Dakota.

Wyoming is a state where the Great Plains gently rise until they meet the Rocky Mountains. Grasslands make up much of the eastern third of the state. Some of the soil is good for growing wheat. The western side of Wyoming is mountainous. Major rivers in the state include the Snake, Bighorn, Powder, Green, North Platte, and Yellowstone Rivers.

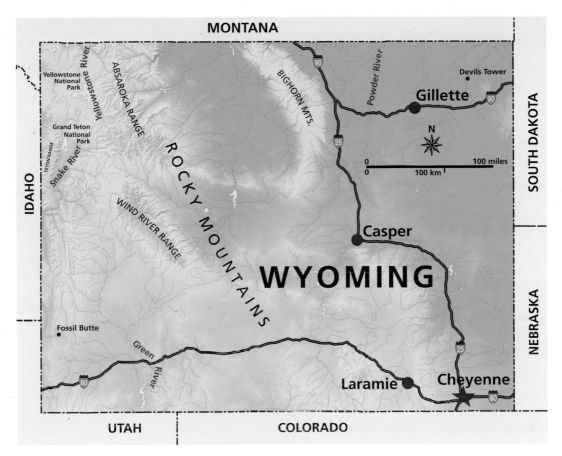

Wyoming's total land and water area is 97,813 square miles (253,335 sq km). It is the 10th-largest state. The state capital is Cheyenne.

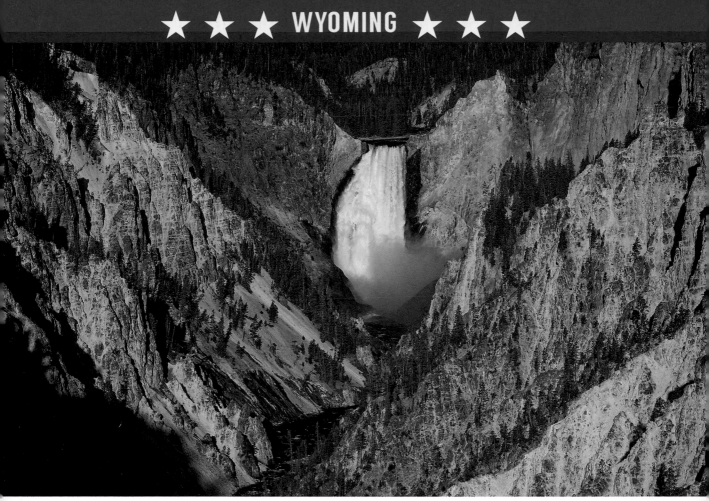

The Lower Falls of the Yellowstone River in Yellowstone National Park.

The Rocky Mountains stretch across much of western Wyoming, generally running from north to south. Wyoming's average elevation is 6,700 feet (2,042 m), second only to Colorado.

There are several sub-ranges of the Rocky Mountains in the state. The Bighorn Mountains are in the north-central part of Wyoming. For many travelers from the east, they are the first big mountains they encounter on their journey across Wyoming. Mountain ranges in the northwest include the Wind River, Absaroka, Gros Ventre, Wyoming, Owl Creek, and Teton Ranges. In southern Wyoming are the Laramie, Medicine Bow, and Sierra Madre Ranges. Wyoming's highest spot is Gannett Peak, which is in the Wind River Range. It soars 13,804 feet (4,207 m) high.

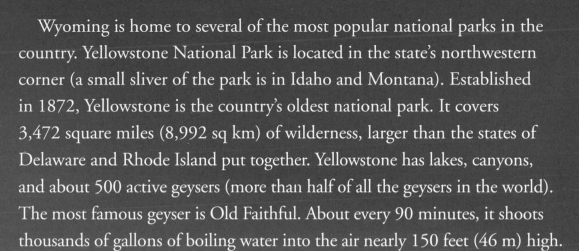

Wyoming is home to several of the most popular national parks in the country. Yellowstone National Park is located in the state's northwestern corner (a small sliver of the park is in Idaho and Montana). Established in 1872, Yellowstone is the country's oldest national park. It covers 3,472 square miles (8,992 sq km) of wilderness, larger than the states of Delaware and Rhode Island put together. Yellowstone has lakes, canyons, and about 500 active geysers (more than half of all the geysers in the world). The most famous geyser is Old Faithful. About every 90 minutes, it shoots thousands of gallons of boiling water into the air nearly 150 feet (46 m) high.

Just south of Yellowstone is Grand Teton National Park, with its many jagged peaks and sparkling lakes. In northeastern Wyoming is Devils Tower. The 1,280-foot (390-m) -tall butte of volcanic rock, and the wilderness surrounding it, became the nation's first national monument in 1906. It played a big role in the 1977 science fiction film *Close Encounters of the Third Kind*.

Devils Tower

11

CLIMATE AND
WEATHER

Elevation affects a state's climate and day-to-day weather. Wyoming's average elevation is 6,700 feet (2,042 m). In the United States, only Colorado is higher. Wyoming's high average elevation results in a cooler climate than most surrounding states. At elevations higher than 6,000 feet (1,829 m), summer temperatures rarely get higher than 100 degrees Fahrenheit (38°C).

Overall, most of Wyoming is arid. Some areas are so dry they receive just 5 inches (13 cm) of rain per year. However, Wyoming's mountains affect how much rain and snow fall. When clouds rise to pass over tall mountains, their moisture condenses and falls as rain or snow. Some mountainous areas in Wyoming receive 45 inches (114 cm) of rain and snow each year.

Buffalo move through a Wyoming snowstorm. The state has a cooler climate than most surrounding states.

Lightning strikes as a rainbow forms during a storm in Sheridan, Wyoming.

Severe weather can sometimes strike the state. Thunderstorms rumble overhead most often in the spring and early summer. The strongest storms bring hail and lightning. Tornadoes are not very common. The state averages about 12 twisters per year, most of them small. Blizzards are a hazard in winter. Heavy snowfalls and high winds can create drifts 25 feet (8 m) or higher, blocking roads sometimes for days.

CLIMATE AND WEATHER

PLANTS AND
ANIMALS

On Wyoming's semi-arid eastern plains, the ground is covered by several kinds of grasses and desert shrubs. The most common shortgrass prairie plants are buffalo grass and blue grama. Mixed-grass prairies include western wheatgrass, Indian ricegrass, blue grama, Sandberg's bluegrass, prairie Junegrass, and upland sedges.

Most of Wyoming's forests are in the mountains, or along rivers and streams. Commonly seen trees are evergreens, including ponderosa pine, lodgepole pine, Douglas fir, and Engelmann spruce. The official state tree is the plains cottonwood.

Millions of acres of Wyoming woodlands are preserved in national parks such as Yellowstone and Grand Teton National Parks, or in national forests, including Bighorn, Bridger-Teton, Medicine Bow, Shoshone, and Targhee National Forests.

A rainstorm over the Absaroka Range.

Elk race across the rolling hills and woodlands of Yellowstone National Park.

Many kinds of colorful wildflowers bloom in Wyoming's prairies and mountain meadows. They include pasqueflower, mariposa lily, arrowhead balsamroot, blue flax, larkspur, prairie coneflower, alpine forget-me-not, and brown-eyed Susan. On the tallest mountains are alpine tundra lichens and mosses. Wyoming's state flower is the Indian paintbrush.

Blue Flax

Mariposa Lily

Indian Paintbrush

PLANTS AND ANIMALS

A grizzly bear mother with cubs in Yellowstone National Park.

Wyoming's grasslands and mountains support much wildlife, including many large mammals. More pronghorn live in Wyoming than any other state. They are among the fastest animals on Earth. Pronghorn have been clocked at up to 53 miles per hour (85 km/hr), leaving predators such as coyotes or wolves far behind in the prairie dust.

Other large mammals found in Wyoming include elk, bighorn sheep, mule deer, and white-tailed deer. Moose, black bears, and grizzly bears live in the northwestern corner of the state. They are often spotted in Yellowstone and Grand Teton National Parks.

Smaller mammals making their homes in Wyoming include cottontail rabbits, jackrabbits, black-footed ferrets, bobcats, skunks, pikas, porcupines, beavers, spotted ground squirrels, foxes, and prairie dogs. Wyoming's official state mammal is the bison. These large herbivores once thundered across the plains by the millions. Today, they are mainly found in northwestern Wyoming in protected parklands. They appear on Wyoming's state flag.

Wild horses race past grazing pronghorn in Wyoming's Adobe Town wilderness area.

Wild horses live on the open range of Wyoming's southwest. Many of them are descended from horses brought to this country by Spanish explorers in the 1600s.

Many kinds of birds can be found soaring through Wyoming's blue skies. They include sage grouse, pheasants, partridges, Canada geese, pelicans, red-tailed hawks, burrowing owls, mountain plovers, upland sandpipers, and wild turkeys. Bald eagles are often seen in western Wyoming. The official state bird is the meadowlark.

There are 22 species of game fish lurking under the surface of Wyoming's lakes, rivers, and streams. They include bass, crappie, perch, bluegill, and walleye, plus several species of trout. The official state fish of Wyoming is the cutthroat trout.

Cutthroat Trout

PLANTS AND ANIMALS

HISTORY

People have lived in the Wyoming area for at least 12,000 years, and perhaps much longer. These Paleo-Indians were the ancient ancestors of today's Native Americans. They were nomads who hunted large animals such as mammoths and bison.

Paleo-Indians hunted bison in Wyoming.

As time passed, native peoples moved in and out of the area. They formed groups or tribes. Just before Europeans arrived in today's Wyoming, the area was settled by several Native American tribes. Many of them lived on the plains. They included the Cheyenne, Sioux, Crow, Arikara, Arapaho, Blackfeet, Nez Percé, Ute, and Shoshone tribes.

A group of Shoshone Native Americans camped by the Wind River Mountains, near today's town of Pinedale, Wyoming.

Mountain man John Colter stands with York. Both were members of the Lewis and Clark Expedition (1804-1806). Later, Colter explored the Yellowstone area.

One of Wyoming's earliest white explorers was John Colter. He had been a member of the Lewis and Clark Expedition. In 1806, Colter set off on his own to explore the Rocky Mountains. He arrived in Wyoming in 1807, stumbling upon the Yellowstone area in the northwest. He marveled at the area's colorful canyons, boiling mud, and steaming geysers. When he wrote about his experiences, many people did not believe him. They nicknamed the area "Colter's Hell." Later expeditions confirmed Yellowstone's wonders. In 1872, the land was set aside as the world's first national park.

John Colter is considered one of the first "mountain men." These rugged men were fur trappers who traveled great distances as they explored the western part of North America. They lived off the land, trapping animals such as beavers and otters. Beaver pelts were prized by hat makers in Europe. Trappers were paid very high prices for their goods. By the early 1800s, mountain men and fur traders were swarming all over the American West, including today's Wyoming.

Some of the most famous mountain men, explorers, and traders came to Wyoming in search of their treasured pelts. They included Kit Carson, Davey Jackson, Jedediah Smith, and Jim Bridger. Nicknamed the "Daniel Boone of the Rockies," it was Bridger who explored the area in 1850 and discovered an easier way across the Rocky Mountains. It is known today as Bridger Pass. It was used by the Union Pacific Railroad when it constructed part of the first transcontinental railroad across Wyoming in 1868. The mountain man also established Fort Bridger in southwestern Wyoming. It began as a trading post, and eventually became a United States Army post in 1858.

Jim Bridger explored the Wyoming area in 1850.

A train passes over Dale Creek Bridge near Sherman, Wyoming. The 650-foot (198-m) -bridge was the longest span built by the Union Pacific Railroad. It was first completed in 1868, but was rebuilt over the years to make it safer.

From the 1840s to the 1860s, hundreds of thousands of people traveled westward across Wyoming. They came on horseback, in covered wagons, and some even on foot. Many used trails such as the Oregon, Overland, Mormon, Bozeman, or Bridger Trails on their way to the West Coast in search of gold or land to farm.

In the late 1860s, railroads were built across Wyoming. New cities and forts supported the railroads, including Cheyenne, Laramie, Rawlins, and Evanston. Instead of passing through, many people decided to stay and settle in Wyoming. Cattle and sheep ranches sprang up all over the area.

With so many new settlers arriving almost daily, Wyoming's Native Americans grew angry that the land they had lived on for hundreds of years was being taken from them. Several battles erupted in the 1850s and 1860s. Some tribes remained peaceful, however. By the 1870s, most of the warfare had ended, and many Native Americans had moved to government reservations.

Francis Warren served as Wyoming's first governor. He later served as the state's second United States senator.

In 1868, Wyoming Territory was organized by the United States Congress. On July 10, 1890, Wyoming became the 44th state in the Union. Businessman and former Army war hero Francis Warren served as the state's first governor. Cheyenne was named the state capital.

In the first years of the 1900s, huge amounts of oil and coal were discovered. Mining became an important industry in the state, in addition to ranching. During World War I (1914-1918), Wyoming was a major supplier of horses to the military.

Warhorses at Fort F.E. Warren near Cheyenne, Wyoming.

For many years, Wyoming was the nation's top producer of uranium.

DANGER RADIOACTIVE MATERIAL

The Great Depression struck in 1929 and lasted throughout much of the 1930s. The economic downturn hit Wyoming hard. Many people lost their jobs, businesses, and homes.

During Word War II (1939-1945), the economy improved. Mining continued to be an important industry. Huge amounts of coal, oil, and natural gas were extracted from the Earth. The radioactive mineral uranium was discovered in Wyoming in 1951. For many years, the state was the nation's top producer of uranium, which is used in nuclear reactors and bombs.

In the last part of the 1900s and early 2000s, Wyoming continued to rely on ranching and mining. Today, it has also expanded its economy to include other kinds of businesses. Tourism is especially important, as millions of people travel to the state each year to experience natural wonders such as Yellowstone and Grand Teton National Parks.

DID YOU KNOW?

Esther Hobart Morris

Estelle Reel Meyer

• Wyoming's nickname is "The Equality State." Women had important rights in Wyoming long before they attained them in other states. Wyoming was the first state to allow women to vote, to hold public offices such as mayor or governor, and to serve on juries. These are all rights we take for granted today, but in the late 1800s, Wyoming's policies were considered to be very progressive and unusual. In 1869, Wyoming's territorial government granted women the right to vote, which was called "female suffrage." That right continued when Wyoming became a state in 1890. In 1870, Esther Hobart Morris of South Pass City was the first woman to be appointed justice of the peace. In 1894, Estelle Reel Meyer was elected to serve as Wyoming's superintendent of public instruction. It was the first time in United States history that a woman was elected to state office. And, in 1924, Nellie Tayloe Ross was elected governor of Wyoming, the first woman governor to ever take office in the United States.

Medicine Wheel

• High in the Bighorn Mountains of north-central Wyoming, there is a mysterious monument made of large stones set in the ground. It is shaped like a wagon wheel, with 28 spokes meeting in the middle. Called Medicine Wheel, it was made by unknown Native Americans hundreds of years ago. It is a symbol of creation. At one time, Crow Indians used it for religious ceremonies. The structure is 75 feet (23 m) in diameter. Today, it is preserved as Medicine Wheel National Historic Landmark.

Independence Rock

• Independence Rock is a granite monolith that rises 136 feet (41 m) out of the surrounding arid plains in central Wyoming. It was a landmark used by pioneers heading west in the mid-1800s along the Oregon Trail. When they stopped to rest, some climbed to the top and carved their names into the stone. Many of these names can still be seen today, giving Independence Rock the nickname "The Great Registry of the Desert." Today, the site is preserved as Independence Rock National Historic Landmark.

DID YOU KNOW?

PEOPLE

Chief Washakie (c. 1804–1900) was a warrior and leader of the Shoshone tribe. Many of his family were killed by tribal warfare when he was young. He grew into a skilled warrior. His talents in battle led him to become a Shoshone chief. He was also a friend of the white settlers. He and his people aided the newcomers when they forded streams, and also helped round up stray cattle. Washakie kept this friendship even though the United States government often took Shoshone land and broke treaties made with the tribe. Washakie's insistence on peace avoided bloodshed. He always sought the best for his people, and he was praised for his treatment of white settlers. He was buried at Wyoming's Fort Washakie with full military honors.

Dick Cheney (1941-) served as vice president of the United States from 2001-2009. He was born in Nebraska, but grew up in Casper, Wyoming. He graduated from the University of Wyoming, earning degrees in political science. Cheney worked as an intern in the Richard Nixon administration. He held several different jobs until becoming White House chief of staff for President Gerald Ford. Cheney was then elected to the U.S. House of Representatives, serving from 1979-1989. His next job was secretary of defense for President George H.W. Bush. In 2001, he became vice president, serving two terms under President George W. Bush.

Nellie Tayloe Ross (1876-1977) was Wyoming's 14th governor. She was also America's first female governor. She was born in Missouri, and went to school in Nebraska. In 1902, she married William Ross. He decided to practice law in the West, so they moved to Cheyenne, Wyoming. William Ross was elected governor of Wyoming in 1922, but died in 1924. In a special election, Nellie was chosen to succeed her husband. She became Wyoming's governor in January 1925. In 1933, President Franklin Roosevelt asked Ross to become the director of the U.S. Mint. The Mint produces money in the United States. Ross was the first woman to hold the job, which she kept until retiring in 1953. Ross lived to the age of 101, traveling, writing, and helping people her entire life.

Buffalo Bill Cody (1846-1917) was a scout, frontiersman, and showman. William Cody was born in Iowa, but spent much of his life on the Great Plains, including Kansas and Wyoming. He worked many jobs to help his family, including trapping and gold mining. He was a rider for the Pony Express, and a soldier during the Civil War. When train tracks were laid across the United States, he hunted for food for the workers on the railroad. He killed many buffalo, earning the nickname "Buffalo Bill." Hc also worked as a scout for the U.S. Army. He began Buffalo Bill's Wild West show in the 1870s. He used his popularity to develop Wyoming. In 1895, he helped found the city of Cody, in northwestern Wyoming, near Yellowstone National Park.

CITIES

Cheyenne is the capital of Wyoming. It is also the state's largest city. Its population is about 63,335. It is located in the southeastern corner of Wyoming. Founded in 1867, the city began when the Union Pacific Railroad was built in the area. It was named after the Cheyenne Native American tribe, which inhabited the region. Settlers soon arrived on the newly built railroad, and the city grew. Today, Cheyenne is a center for government, transportation, and education. The city is proud of its Western heritage. The Cheyenne Frontier Days Old West Museum has art exhibits, historical artifacts (including a collection of horse-drawn carriages), and a research center. The city's biggest festival is Cheyenne Frontier Days. Held yearly since 1897, the Western-themed celebration includes parades, music, rodeos, and dancing.

Casper is Wyoming's second-largest city. Its population is about 60,285. It is located in east-central Wyoming. It began as a trading post for settlers traveling west on the Oregon Trail in the 1840s and 1850s. Later, it became a military post for the U.S. Army. The city is named for Lieutenant Caspar Collins. The young man died during a battle with Native Americans in 1865. A misspelling caused the name to change to "Casper" when the city was founded in 1888. At first, Casper was a lawless town filled with rowdy cowboys. Eventually, new businesses moved in, and the city grew. In 1889, oil was discovered in the area. The city became a major center for oil refining. Today, Casper remains a supplier of oil, natural gas, and coal. Uranium mining, retail, banking, and health care are also important.

CITIES

Gillette is Wyoming's third-largest city. Its population is about 32,649. It is located in the northeastern part of the state. Huge deposits of coal and oil are located in the area. Residents of Gillette call it the "Energy Capital of the Nation." Wyoming is the country's number-one supplier of coal. Mines in the Gillette area produce much of that coal. Oil and uranium are also extracted. The Wright Centennial Museum has large collections featuring pioneer history, including chuck wagons, the cowboy's kitchen on the range. Gillette is a popular base for hunters, who pursue big game such as pronghorn and deer on the Wyoming plains. Nearby is Devils Tower National Monument.

Laramie is Wyoming's fourth-largest city. Its population is about 32,158. It is located in the southeastern corner of the state, just west of the capital of Cheyenne. Laramie was founded in the 1860s, when railroads were built in the area. It was a wild, lawless frontier town at first. In time, more settlers came, new businesses appeared, and the town grew. Today, important industries include agriculture (especially ranching), forest products, transportation, tourism, and education. In 1886, Laramie became the home of the University of Wyoming. It enrolls about 14,000 students. Its popular Geological Museum displays thousands of mineral and fossil specimens, including the skeleton of "Big Al" the *Allosaurus*, who lived about 150 million years ago.

TRANSPORTATION

There are 29,024 miles (46,710 km) of public roadways in Wyoming. Interstate I-80 is a major east-west route across the state. It roughly follows the same path taken by the historic first transcontinental railroad in southern Wyoming. It passes through the cities of Cheyenne, Laramie, and Evanston. Interstate I-25 runs generally north and south across the state, passing through Cheyenne and Casper. Interstate I-90 is in the northeastern corner of Wyoming. It passes through the cities of Gillette, Buffalo, and Sheridan.

One of the most famous roadways in America is U.S. Route 212, also known as the Beartooth Scenic Highway. It begins near the northeastern entrance of Yellowstone National Park. Part of the highway is also in neighboring Montana. The roadway is filled with hairpin turns and spectacular, dizzying mountain scenery. Its highest point is Beartooth Pass, which climbs to 10,947 feet (3,337 m).

Beartooth Scenic Highway

There are 4 freight railroads in Wyoming operating on 1,860 miles (2,993 km) of track. The most common product hauled by rail is, by far, coal. Wyoming is the nation's number-one supplier of coal. Other Wyoming products hauled by train include chemicals, minerals, cement, plus sand and gravel. There are no passenger trains currently operating in Wyoming.

Nine commercial airports serve Wyoming. The state's busiest airport is Jackson Hole Airport. It is located in Grand Teton National Park. It is the only airport in the country that operates inside a national park.

Coal trains move Wyoming's number-one product across the state.

35

NATURAL
RESOURCES

There are about 11,600 farms that operate in the state of Wyoming. Together, they occupy 30.4 million acres (12.3 million ha) of land. That is 49 percent, or almost half, of the state's total land area.

There is a good reason one of Wyoming's nicknames is "The Cowboy State." Nearly 90 percent of agricultural land is used for grazing cattle or sheep. About 65 percent of all Wyoming's agriculture income comes from cattle. Other livestock raised includes sheep, hogs, and horses. Wyoming ranks third nationwide in wool production.

A cattle drive near Laramie, Wyoming.

Harvested bales of hay wait for pickup in a Wyoming field.

The most valuable crops raised in Wyoming include hay, barley, corn, beans, wheat, sugar beets, and oats. The biggest wheat fields are in the southeastern corner of the state.

Deep under Wyoming's crust are rich deposits of minerals. The most valuable are coal, oil, and natural gas. Wyoming is the nation's top producer of coal. It is burned to produce electricity in large power plants. Most of Wyoming's coal is found in the Powder River Basin, in the northeastern part of the state. Wyoming has an estimated 68.7 billion tons (62.3 billion metric tons) of coal left in the ground, enough to last for decades.

Wyoming has the largest supply of trona in the world. It is a mineral used to make paper, soap, glass, water softeners, and medicines. Other minerals found in Wyoming include limestone, gypsum, and bentonite clay.

NATURAL RESOURCES

INDUSTRY

Wyoming's biggest manufacturing businesses are related to its two most important industries: mining and agriculture. Large firms process raw materials such as coal and oil. Many other businesses support these industries, including the makers of heavy machinery, construction equipment, and

An oil pump jack on the Wyoming plains.

oil rigs and pumps. Wyoming manufacturers also produce chemicals, fertilizers, food products, wool products, glass, and clay products.

Wyoming's economy depends heavily on energy prices. As these prices change, the state's economy changes as well. In recent decades, Wyoming has tried to diversify its economy so that it isn't affected so much by any one industry. The service industry has become increasingly important. Instead of making products, service industry companies sell services to other businesses and consumers. The service industry includes businesses such as banking, financial services, health care, restaurants, and tourism.

Four million people per year visit Yellowstone National Park. Old Faithful Geyser, which erupts every 60-110 minutes, is the most popular attraction. Water and steam shoot to a varying height of 106 to 184 feet (32–56 m).

Tourism has been a bright spot in Wyoming's economy. More than 10 million people travel to the state yearly to visit parks such as Yellowstone and Grand Teton National Parks, or to attend festivals such as Cheyenne Frontier Days. Tourists spend about $3.3 billion in the state each year, enough to support 32,000 jobs.

SPORTS

There are no professional major league sports teams based in Wyoming. However, many people closely follow their town's high school sports teams, or the teams of the University of Wyoming in Laramie. The men's teams of the university are called the Cowboys, while the women's teams are called the Cowgirls. They play in a variety of sports, including track, swimming, and rugby. Football and basketball are the most popular.

Wyoming's wide-open spaces are ideal for outdoor sports lovers. Tourists enjoy visiting working cattle ranches, called dude ranches. They can try their hands at horse riding and rounding up stray livestock. Both visitors and residents alike enjoy hiking, backpacking, camping, hunting, fishing, and wildlife viewing. People with an adventurous streak like whitewater rafting, mountain climbing, hang gliding, or exploring the state's many caves.

Adventurers take a whitewater rafting trip on Wyoming's Snake River.

Thanks to the state's many cattle ranches, Western heritage is an important part of Wyoming life. Rodeo is a very popular sport, both at the high school level and professionally. In fact, rodeo is the official state sport of Wyoming.

The rodeo at the Cheyenne Frontier Days festival is nicknamed "The Daddy of 'em All." Exciting fans since 1897 with rip-roarin' action, it is the world's largest outdoor rodeo. Events include bronc riding, steer wrestling, barrel racing, and bull riding.

SPORTS

ENTERTAINMENT

The culture of the American West is alive and well in Wyoming. Residents of the state are proud of their traditions. Cheyenne Frontier Days has been held each summer in the capital since 1897. The multi-day celebration features the word's biggest outdoor rodeo, as well as parades, musical acts, dancing, a chuck wagon cook-off, an old frontier town, a Native American

Frontier Days participants take part in a parade.

village, arts and crafts, and even an air show. More than 260,000 people come to Cheyenne each year to attend the festival.

The Jackson Hole Fall Arts Festival attracts thousands of art lovers each year to the town of Jackson, just south of Grand Teton National Park. It features fine art that highlights the landscape and wildlife of the Rocky Mountains.

The Buffalo Bill Center of the West features artifacts such as a full-size wagon, Bill Cody's buffalo hide coat, and amazing Western art.

The Buffalo Bill Center of the West, in Cody, has one of the largest and most prestigious collections of Western artifacts and fine art in the world. It holds five complete museums, plus a library. Many of the exhibits trace the life and times of William "Buffalo Bill" Cody, the legendary scout and showman. There are also world-class exhibits highlighting the Plains Indians, Western fine art, natural history, and antique firearms. The Buffalo Bill Center of the West is a must-see stop for many people traveling through Cody on their way west to nearby Yellowstone National Park.

TIMELINE

10,000 BC—Paleo-Indians arrive in the Wyoming area, hunting large game such as mammoths and bison.

Pre-1800s—Cheyenne, Sioux, Crow, Arikara, Arapaho, Blackfeet, Nez Percé, Ute, and Shoshone tribes settle in Wyoming.

1807—Mountain man John Colter explores Wyoming and the Yellowstone area.

1834—Fur traders establish Fort Laramie.

1843—Fort Bridger is established.

1840s-1860s—Wyoming becomes a crossroads for people traveling west.

1860s—Railroads are built across Wyoming.

1868—Wyoming Territory established.

1872—Yellowstone National Park established, the first national park in the United States.

1890—Wyoming becomes the 44th state in the Union.

1925—Nellie Tayloe Ross is sworn in as Wyoming's governor. She becomes the nation's first female governor.

1941-1945—Prisoner-of-war camps and Japanese-American relocation centers are set up in Wyoming during World War II.

1951—Uranium is discovered in Wyoming.

2009—Wyoming resident Dick Cheney retires from politics after serving two terms as vice president of the United States.

2015—The University of Wyoming Cowboys men's basketball team wins the Mountain West Conference Basketball Tournament and appears in the NCAA Men's Division I Basketball Tournament.

GLOSSARY

ARAPAHO
A Native American tribe that lived on the plains of Wyoming and Colorado.

ARID
A climate that has very little rain or snow.

BLACKFEET
A Native American tribe that lived on the plains. They often used ashes to stain their moccasins black.

CHEYENNE
A Great Plains Native American tribe. The capital of Wyoming is named after the Cheyenne.

ELEVATION
The height of a location, based on how far from sea level it is.

GEYSER
A spring that shoots up hot water with explosive force from time to time. Old Faithful is among several famous geysers found in Wyoming's Yellowstone National Park.

LEWIS AND CLARK EXPEDITION
An exploration of western North America, led by Meriwether Lewis and William Clark, from 1804-1806.

MOUNTAIN MEN
Hunters, guides, and explorers who traveled in the wilds of Wyoming and lived off the land.

Nez Percé

A tribe of Native Americans who lived in the mountain valleys of Wyoming, and who traveled seasonally to other areas.

Pony Express

A way of delivering mail from 1860-1861. A relay of riders delivered letters from Missouri to California.

Shoshone

A Native American tribe that lived in western Wyoming. Sacagawea, of the Lewis and Clark Expedition, was probably a Shoshone tribe member.

Sioux

An alliance of Great Plains Native American tribes who spoke three related languages: Dakota, Nakota, and Lakota.

Transcontinental Railroad

An American railroad line that stretched from the Atlantic Ocean to the Pacific Ocean, across the continent. The railroad being built westward (the Union Pacific Railroad) met the railroad going east (the Central Pacific Railroad) at Promontory Summit, near Salt Lake City, in 1869. Part of the railroad was built across southern Wyoming.

World War I

A war that was fought in Europe from 1914 to 1918, involving countries around the world. The United States entered the war in April 1917.

World War II

A conflict that was fought from 1939 to 1945, involving countries around the world. The United States entered the war after Japan bombed the American naval base at Pearl Harbor, in Oahu, Hawaii, on December 7, 1941.

INDEX